Comprehension Speed Reading: Learn Techniques to Read Faster and Comprehend More

Dedicated to the many supportive people in my life.

It's been said it takes a village to raise a child; and it's true.

To the villagers, I say thank you.

Your Free Gift

I want to show my appreciation for supporting my work so I've put together a little gift for you.

http://comprehensionspeedreading.gr8.com

Just visit the link above to download it now!

I know you will love this gift.

Thanks!

David A. Daniels

Timber Publishing

Contents

Introduction

Some people say that nowadays we're required to read less and less, but the truth is far from this statement. We read more than we even realize: from the moment we open our emails in the morning to procrastinating on Facebook at work. We read pamphlets, articles, online material including the news, and sometimes we even read books.

And yet, how *fast* do we read and perhaps even more important, how much do we *comprehend* what we read?

Speed reading is frequently misunderstood. We tend to believe that you either need some sort of "supernatural" talent to do this, or that if you speed read you're missing out on much of the information as you read.

As you will see though, speed reading goes beyond bouncing one's eyes on a sheet of paper just for the sake of "reading". Speed reading can be extremely useful when done the right way and this is precisely what this book aims to do: to show you how you can read faster and understand more through simple techniques that actually work.

If you are searching for a miracle book that will teach you how to study faster, how to get through your business papers fasters or how to read Tolstoy's *War and Peace* in two hours because you have to sit in an exam tomorrow morning, this is not what you need.

This is a book that will put all the tools of speed reading into your hands, so that you can use them going forward. Remember that whether or not you actually decide to apply the advice in your own life is entirely up to you! However, this is a skill that, if gained, will benefit your life.

We will start with the reasons why speed reading can be extremely beneficial in your life and you will find out why your motivation behind learning how to read faster is so important.

We will proceed by showing you how to assess yourself, how to spot the things that stop you from reading faster and then how to improve yourself in all of these areas. Last, but not least, we will show you a few tips that will help you determine which texts can be read at a fast speed and which ones should not (because yes, not everything should be speed-read).

By the end of this book, you will hold the tools which make great readers from a perspective considering both the speed you can read and the amount you can comprehend.

Congratulations! You have made an extremely important step towards becoming one of these readers as well! Reading more will help you grow faster personally and will increase your potential – so you've really got nothing to lose!

Chapter 1: Why Speed Reading?

You could simply go on with your life without learning how to read faster – and that would be *fine*. But, people who want to excel at what they do *want* to read faster for a very simple reason: it provides them with more information.

Let's put it this way: The average reader goes through one book (fiction or non-fiction) in about two weeks (give or take). That makes for around 26 books every year – and this number is valid for someone who is consistent with his/her two-week book. Doubling your reading speed will automatically double your annual number of books read, to 56 books a year, (if you're average). You're not average though, an 'average' person wouldn't have picked up this book. You might feel like a slow reader now, but it's certainly possible to more than double your reading speed. Increasing your reading speed along with comprehension will allow you to consume more material, more books – and that makes for more knowledge.

Aside from the fact that you will gain more knowledge in less time, there are other benefits to learning how to speed-read. For instance, speed reading comes with a high level of concentration and improving your ability to focus will be beneficial in almost every single area of your life.

Speed reading can help you study faster, which means you will have more time to read the things you would like to read or do things you have always wanted to do. For those of you in college, the large amount of books you have to read every single semester can be overwhelming – but speed reading can help you get through them faster.

As you can see, there are many things that can motivate you to learn how to read faster. Motivation plays an important role in keeping up with your speed reading progress, so make sure you always know *why* you are doing this. Why have you opened this book? Why do you want to learn how to read faster? Why do you want to push your limits?

Forgive the overused analogy, but learning to speed-read is similar to weight loss or learning a foreign language: the *why* gets you *there* eventually. For instance, some want to lose weight because they want to fit into a smaller jean size. Other people have to lose weight because their health is in danger while others want to lose weight (or add muscle) simply because it improves their self-confidence. This works the same with learning how to speed-read: your motivation will get you through the harsher times and it will help you "surface" victorious.

So, why speed reading?

Because information is power. Because you want to be at the top of the pyramid. Because it is a new challenge. Because you have a long list of books you really want to read. Because you want to learn more. Because studying for college is time-consuming. Because your business needs it. Because *you* need it!

There are millions of reasons *why*. But, you have to pick the reasons that fit you best and to stick to them throughout the entire "transformation" process. Same as running a marathon, learning to read faster will be a challenge and you need your *whys* to be well defined. That way when it gets tough and when you are pushed out of your comfort zone you won't feel like quitting; instead you'll simply push through it with determination and end up with another great skill!

Chapter 2: Where Do You Stand?

In the previous chapter we made an analogy between speed reading and weight loss or fitness training. Keeping this analogy in mind will help you better understand why certain steps have to be taken and this includes the very first step; knowing where you stand.

When you start training (for weight loss, body building or any other reason), one of the first things your trainer will do is assess where you stand at that moment and what your physical condition is *now*. This works the same with speed reading. You should first and foremost assess your current reading speed to know where you stand and to be able to establish a goal to be achieved.

How do you do that?

There is more than one way to calculate your words-per-minute (WPM) rate. However, we've provided three speed reading tests in the appendix of this book, which are approximately 700 words long, to use in assessing your current reading rate; and then return to and use to assess your improvement as you use the techniques provided in this book. Each 700-word reading segment also has an accompanying comprehension test, which follows each reading segment within the appendix of this book.

To assess your reading rate, first set a stopwatch and time yourself reading one of the 700-word reading segments. While reading it, do so at your regular pace. Don't try to rush your reading or beat the clock. We're assessing where your reading speed is now. Then look at the *Speed Reading Rate* chart provided, at the end of this chapter and in the appendix, to find the amount of time it took you to read the segment. Then look to the column to the left which will give you your words-per-minute reading rate. Once you've figured out your starting WPM reading rate, then take the *Speed Reading Assessment Test*, associated with the reading segment you've just finished reading. Answer the test questions, and then check your work by looking up the answers provided in the appendix following the assessment tests. Again, make sure to be *honest* about it – you are NOT allowed to go back and search for your answers in the text! There are ten questions provided for each test, making each question worth 10%. Therefore, if you answered 8 of the questions correctly, then you achieved a score of 80%. Now go back to the *Speed Reading Rate* table, look up your words-per-minute (WPM) rate, and then move to the left until you find the column under the score you achieved on the *Speed Reading Assessment Test*, there you will find your Effective Words Per Minute (EWPM) reading rate.

Your EWPM is the number we suggest you use as your starting number. Why? Well, simply put we want you to use the techniques in this book to read fast, but also comprehend more. Being a fast reader, but one who doesn't really comprehend what is read is ineffective. We want to improve your speed and effectiveness when it comes to reading!

An average person typically reads around 200 EWPM. Anything over 300 EWPM is considered great, and an excellent speed reading rate is anything over 700 EWPM.

Where do you stand? Average, below average? Don't worry about it if you are. Celebrate the fact that you're taking action to improve yourself and learn a new skill! If you did not get a very high number, this can be improved (and we will show you how later in this book!).

Even more than that, do not worry if your WPM or your EWPM is average – that is perfectly normal. In fact, most people have an average reading speed and comprehension level – and this includes the brightest minds out there. Doctors, lawyers, engineers – most of them do not have a very high reading speed. But imagine the huge number of things all of them *could* do if they did have a high EWPM! Imagine what you'll be able to do with a higher EWPM reading rate.

Mircea Eliade was a speed reader, for example. He read everything he could get his hands on. Sometimes, he even read books in the bookstore without having to buy them. What did he accomplish with his new ability? Well, he was the first man who ever thought of writing an entire History of Religions.

Now, you may not aim at the same things as he did, but speed reading will definitely push you forward with your dreams, with your career and with all the things you have always wanted to learn about the world in which we live.

It is important to know where you stand right now, yes. But even more than that, it is important to know how to improve. It is important to *want* to improve and to *work your way* toward your goal. You can do this and remember it is important to keep maintain a positive and motivated mindset! With the right attitude and dedication, you'll definitely reach your goal of reading faster and comprehending more!

SPEED READING RATE

Time (Minutes)	Words Per Minute (WPM)	Effective Words Per Minute (EWPM)									
		10%	20%	30%	40%	50%	60%	70%	80%	90%	100%
1.00	1,447	145	289	434	579	724	868	1,013	1,158	1,302	1,447
1.25	1,158	116	232	347	463	579	695	811	926	1,042	1,158
1.50	965	97	193	290	386	483	579	676	772	869	965
1.75	827	83	165	248	331	414	496	579	661	744	827
2.00	724	72	145	217	289	362	434	507	579	652	724
2.25	643	64	129	193	257	322	386	450	514	579	643
2.50	579	58	116	174	232	290	347	405	463	521	579
2.75	526	53	105	158	210	263	316	368	421	473	526
3.00	482	48	96	145	193	241	289	337	386	434	482
3.25	445	45	89	134	178	223	267	312	356	401	445
3.50	413	41	83	124	165	207	248	289	331	372	413
3.75	386	39	77	116	154	193	232	270	309	347	386
4.00	362	36	72	109	145	181	217	253	289	326	362
4.25	340	34	68	102	136	170	204	238	272	306	340
4.50	322	32	64	97	129	161	193	225	257	290	322
4.75	305	31	61	92	122	153	183	214	244	275	305
5.00	289	29	58	87	116	145	174	202	232	260	289
5.25	276	28	55	83	110	138	165	193	220	248	276
5.50	263	26	53	79	105	132	158	184	210	237	263
5.75	252	25	50	76	101	126	151	176	201	227	252
6.00	241	24	48	72	96	121	145	169	193	217	241
6.25	232	23	46	70	93	116	139	162	185	209	232
6.50	223	22	45	67	89	112	134	156	178	201	223
6.75	214	21	43	64	86	107	129	150	171	193	214
7.00	207	20	41	62	83	104	124	145	165	186	207

Chapter 3: What Stops You From Being a Champion Reader?

Now that you know what your reading speed is, you may wonder what it is that stops you from being a true champion reader. Knowing what makes you *lag* is absolutely crucial because it will help you eliminate the issues and focus on improvement.

Below, you will be presented with some of the most commonly encountered obstacles which are common contributors to people reading slower and/or comprehending less.

Poor Peripheral Vision

One of the many potential causes why you are not reading at your best speed is bad peripheral vision. As you will later see, speed reading relies a lot on this and it will be crucial for you to find a way to improve it.

One of the simplest exercises you can try is sitting and looking straight ahead. Fixate your eyes on a point as far left as you can possibly see and then move it to a point at the same height in the right corner of your eyes. Practice this back and forth movement about 10 times and try to push your vision even further each time. Also, keep in mind the fact that the speed at which you do this should be as fast-paced as you can manage, but that the movement should also be smooth.

Reading Word-for-Word

When we start reading in primary school, we are taught to do it word-for-word. Many of us stick to this habit as adults as well, but the truth is that this is one of the worst enemies speed reading can have.

Why is this habit so bad for your reading speed? When you read word-for-word, your eyes stop each and every time.

Every stop your eyes make should be translated as ½ of a second. Therefore, a word-for-word reader will need 7 seconds to read this sentence. When you read more words at once, your eyes stop fewer times, which means that your total reading time will be lower. A very fast reader will only stop his/her eyes twice for the above-mentioned sentence, which means he/she will only need one second to read it through. That's 7 times faster than a slow reader!

There is yet another reason for which reading word-for-word is not a good choice. Think of this: your thoughts don't form *one word at a time*, so why should your reading?

Sub-Vocalization

You know the tiny voice at the back of your head, reading you the words in the books? That's "sub-vocalization" and it is one of the top reasons people don't read as fast as they can. We speak slower than we think and that voice is not doing anything else than slowing you down by "uttering" the words. You don't need it! As you get farther into this book and as you start learning some of the most important techniques that help you read faster, you will see that voice slowly disappear.

Back-Skipping

Back-skipping is a problem many readers encounter, especially when they are reading texts that are a bit more difficult. Basically, this problem will make you return to text you have previously read because you either don't remember something or because something doesn't make sense. This issue is overcome with the help of the techniques that are described throughout the following pages of this book.

Tired Eyes

Another issue which makes many people read at a much slower pace than their maximum potential is the fact that their eyes are tired. When you read, your eyes move from left to right very fast, so it is natural that they get tired at times. Make sure you take a break every once in a while to rest your eyes. Ideally, you should take a break every 30 minutes which will not only allow you to rest your eyes, but will also help you memorize more of what you have just read. Studies show that people are more likely to remember the first and the last thing they have read. This means that if you take a short break from reading every half hour, then you'll likely remember four points well. Therefore taking short breaks improves your comprehension. Taking a short break every fifteen minutes should therefore allow you to remember eight points you've read well. Taking 'breaks' may seem like a hindrance to reading quickly, but we want to read *and* comprehend what we're reading. So take a little break every fifteen to thirty minutes. It could be as simple as standing up and stretching or simply closing and gently rubbing your tired eyes. Try it out and see how it works for you!

Poor Vision

We have talked about how poor peripheral vision can influence your reading speed. However, what many people don't actually think of is that their eyes' health can be one of the major factors contributing to their lower reading speeds. Get your eyes checked regularly, wear your glasses and make sure to change them when the doctor prescribes it! Also, if you read on a computer or mobile device, make sure to get glasses with anti-reflection properties, because this will also protect the health of your eyes.

The Environment

The environment in which you read can be an important factor. Generally speaking, if you want to read faster, you should find a place that makes you feel comfortable (but not *too* comfortable) and where it is unlikely that you will be distracted.

For instance, if you want to study for an exam, avoid the dorm because it is very probable that you will be distracted. Avoid the lounge room as well, because you may feel tempted to watch TV or take a nap. As surprising as this may sound, avoid the library too. Very frequently, libraries are too warm, too cozy and too distracting because there are many people wandering around. Instead, go for an empty classroom – it will be quiet, there will be nobody to disturb you and it will also be comfortable *enough*.

Lack of Sleep

When your grandmother told you about beauty sleep, she knew very well just how important those eight hours of sleeping every night are (and not just for your *beauty!*). Sure, you may feel that you are increasing your productivity by staying up late, but the truth is that this will affect the way in which you perform the next day. Before you know it, you will be part of an endless *cycle* that makes you feel constantly tired.

Not sleeping enough can affect your power to focus and this can affect your reading speed. It is much more likely that you will get distracted, sleepy or simply that you will be unable to comprehend what you read, which will consequently reduce your speed as well.

Bottom line? Think of how many hours you need to sleep per night to feel your best and then try to get in those hours of sleep! If it doesn't work any other way, think of a particular time you should be going to sleep and stick to that schedule.

Not Enough Vocabulary

Having the background knowledge and the necessary vocabulary to understand a text will prevent you from back-skipping and from reading word-for-word. While you will definitely not be able to memorize all the words in the English language, there are some things you can do.

The very best you can do in order to avoid back-skipping because you don't understand a particular word is to try to determine its meaning from the context. This may not always work, but at least the next time you encounter the same word, you will be more familiar with it.

Also, learning how words are generally composed can be helpful. For instance, the prefix "post" means "after", so every word that is composed with this should mean "after something". Examples include "post-meridian", "post-apocalyptic" and so on.

The worst thing you can do is memorize dictionary words by heart. Most likely, you will not remember much this way and you will simply be wasting your time with something that is just not productive.

Furthermore, looking up words in the dictionary while you're reading will slow you down – so try to keep this to a minimum.

Not Enough Practice

Going back to the analogy with training, speed reading is something you practice continuously. Not practicing enough will slow you down and will not improve your speed much. So remember to practice, practice, practice!

Ideally, you should read as much as possible every single day (and you should try to apply the techniques described in this book when appropriate). Considering the fact that you are probably very busy (like most of us), you may feel that you don't have much time at your disposal. However, the truth is that you can find a lot of spare time to practice on your speed reading skills if you set your mind to it.

Read on the bus. Read during lunch breaks. Read before or after work (for instance, you can come in early and you can leave later). Read whenever you get the chance – but don't leave one day without at least 30 minutes of practice. It's likely you're already reading for 30 minutes a day between all the material you're already consuming, so just start using the techniques here and soon you'll be able to read more!

In time, this will become a habit (and a very healthy one I might add) and make it fun, then you'll find it easy to make time to do something you like!

Not Going Beyond Your Comfort Level

We all feel comfortable reading at a specific pace. But, if you want to become a "professional" reader, you will have to leave your comfort level behind and constantly push forward.

Again, the analogy with sports: professional runners or bodybuilders would not get very far if they stayed within their comfort zone. They are constantly training to push their limits farther and farther – so they can achieve true success!

Also, don't be "scared" of reading faster. This is not something that you "enable" once and then live with for the rest of your life. Once you master the techniques described later, you should be able to turn your speed reading skill "on" and "off" whenever you choose. In fact, as you will later discover, this is something that is highly advisable, since not all texts should be read the same way.

These are some of the problems that make people read at a much slower pace than what they actually can read. Keep them in mind and, if you find yourself doing any of these, try to catch yourself when you're doing it and to correct it. The most difficult bad reading habits to get rid of are the sub-vocalization and back-skipping, but in time, you will learn how to manage these and to keep yourself focused on reading faster *and* understanding what you read.

Chapter 4: Speed Reading Exercises and Techniques

As mentioned before, speed reading is something you will practice. Bear in mind, the exercises described here are not *a skill*, but something that can help you gain this skill if you practice enough.

Most of these speed reading exercises will feel ridiculously easy at first – and in one way or another, they are. Speed reading is not rocket science. You don't have to learn quantum physics to read faster. You don't have to change every belief in your life to gain this skill.

But you will have to get out of your comfort zone – and that is precisely where most of those who try to pick up speed reading fail. When things become slightly more difficult, they quit.

The first tip of advice to keep in mind when it comes to learning how to read faster (or learning anything new, for that matter) is to never quit. Apply the following advice and practice these exercises and you will see yourself improving as you move along.

Pacing

This is one of the most frequently encountered speed reading exercises and you may already be familiar with it. Stated simply, pacing means *following* the words you are reading by using your fingers or a card. It is very likely that you have done this before. For instance, some teachers ask their pupils to trace the words they are reading when they first learn the alphabet.

Believe it or not, this simple method can go a very long way when it comes to improving your reading speed. There are multiple ways in which you can do this, and each of them is suitable for certain types of texts.

Left Pointing

Left pointing pacing is the exercise that you will use your index finger (on either hand) and will start at the left margin of the text. Start by placing your index on the left part of the page, at the beginning of it. Read by moving your eyes towards the right side and by moving downwards with your finger, in a vertical line. To push your eyes to move faster, try to move your finger downwards at a faster pace as well.

This method is suitable both for narrower columns of texts (such as those encountered in newspapers for example) and for wider columns as well (such as those in novels). Left pointing is extremely useful because it trains your eyes to follow the line faster. Furthermore, *it is very helpful when you are tired and when you want to keep yourself focused*.

Right Pointing

This exercise is very much similar to the one described above, the only difference is that you will be placing your finger on the right margin of the text. The "trick" here is that you will be "targeting" at your finger, which will be placed at the end of the line (instead of "returning" to the finger). Try both of them and see which one fits you the best and which one feels more comfortable to you.

Center Pointing

Again, this method is also similar to both of the ones described above. However, your index finger will be placed at the center of the first line. Unlike the other two methods though, this method will not work very well with wide columns of texts because your peripheral vision may not be able to "catch" everything that is on the left and right sides of your finger.

Snake Pointing

This method is probably the slowest one of all, but it can still be helpful when you need to keep yourself focused (and not so much to speed yourself up). Start by placing your index finger at the beginning of the first line. Move it across and under this line and then quickly move it to the beginning of the 4th or 5th line underneath the first line. Repeat this. While you move your finger, try to make your eyes move as fast as possible to "meet" with it. Again, this technique works better with narrow columns and not so much with wider columns.

Three-Finger Pointing

When you are dealing with wider columns of text, this method can be quite useful. Keep your index finger, your middle finger and your ring finger together and curl the other two in your palm. Use this group of fingers the same way that you used your index finger in the above-mentioned techniques. You will rapidly be moving along the lines with your fingers and this will push your eyes to read faster as well. Although this particular method may make you feel a bit "dizzy", it can be quite efficient at the same time too.

Double-Pointing

Again, if you want to read texts spread across wide columns as fast as possible, this pacing method will come in handy. You will use both of your index fingers – one will be placed at the left side of the column and the other one will be placed at the right side. You will move both of the fingers downwards as you read every line. This way, you will keep your eyes focused on the text and you will avoid back-skipping.

Card Pointing

If you want to focus more on the reading part without being concerned about how you move your fingers, a blank card can be very useful. Furthermore, the straight edge of the card will help you stay focused even more than the methods described before.

Start by placing the card above the first line of your text. As you read through each text, move the card one line lower. The trick with this technique is using a card that is as wide as your text, so that you keep your eyes on the lines only.

Card Cutout

This technique is not as frequently encountered, but some people find it helpful, so you may want to try it out as well. Instead of using a blank card and tracing it on top of the lines you are reading, use a card with a cutout part in it. The cutout part should be as wide as the text. This should help you keep your eyes on the line you are on at the moment without back-skipping or moving your eyes off the page.

These are just some of the speed reading techniques out there. Of course, there are others as well – but these ones are some of the most efficient and easy to use. Keep it in mind: they are "tools" on your path to being a speed reader, so make sure to use those with which you feel comfortable as often as possible.

Keywords

It has already been established that reading word-for-word is not a good option. Looking for keywords, however, is one of the most commonly recommended speed reading techniques.

You may not be fully aware of this, but most of what we read are not important words. Link words, "fluff" words and many other words are there just to give a sentence its structure, and not so much its meaning. Reading through them very swiftly and focusing more on the so-called "keywords" (those words that add actual meaning to a sentence) should speed you up as well.

When it comes to this technique, many people fear that they are not "finding the right keyword", and this slows them down instead of making them read faster. If you feel the similarly, then you should stop worrying. You *are naturally finding the keywords*, so simply allow your eyes to move on and allow your brain to take in the information you are "picking up".

Also, one thing you should definitely pay attention to is the word "not". This tiny three-letter word can change the entire meaning of a sentence, so make sure not to rule it out simply because it's small. Train your eyes to spot it by looking at a text and searching (as fast as possible) for this word. Practicing this exercise as often as you can will eventually teach your eyes to naturally pick up "not" so that you grasp the actual meaning of a sentence without back-skipping.

All in all, the keyword technique can be extremely helpful if you want to read faster. It will speed you up, it will help you reduce sub-vocalization and it will also help you expand your peripheral vision in a natural way. Furthermore, reading the keywords will also improve your concentration levels and it will help you comprehend more of the texts you are reading (precisely because keywords carry more "weight" in a text). At first, it will feel a bit uncomfortable not to read every single word in a sentence, but you will soon learn to do this successfully.

Chunking

If the keyword method doesn't work for you, the chunking one should do it. Chunking refers to picking up groups of words that naturally form a thought in your head. As it was mentioned before, people normally think in groups of words (and not word-by-word), so this should feel more natural for you.

The main impediment when it comes to chunking the words together is not the fact that your brain doesn't find it natural, but the fact that you are "trained" from a very early age to *not* do this. When you first learned how to read and write, you were reading one word at a time (and most likely, speaking it out as well). As you grew up, you left the talking part behind (some never leave it completely behind), but you kept the word-by-word pattern with you.

Chunking words should feel easier than finding keywords. Basically, you just have to look at a text and mentally split it into smaller pieces that make some sort of sense when taken individually. Take the following text as an example:

When Mary opened the door/, she knew very well/ what she was going to find there/: an empty room/. A room she hadn't visited/ in a very long time/. The room of her childhood'/.

Keep in mind that the size of each chunk of words is not as important as the fact that it should make sense to you. For instance, you may have chosen to split the text above differently – and that would be more than fine as long as it makes sense to you.

Also, remember that a chunk that is too large will not be efficient (as it will probably push you to back-skip and read word-for-word as well). At the same time, a chunk of text that is too small will lower your comprehension level, so make sure to keep it balanced.

Keyword Chunking

Mixing the keyword and chunking methods often works really well. Some of the very fast readers out there do it and they believe it is helpful. Basically, you can pick up chunks of words and keywords at the same time. This will help you increase your speed, improve your peripheral vision and your concentration as well; so there is really no reason not to utilize this technique.

How do you know this (or any of the "keyword" and "chunking" methods) is useful and suitable for you?

You should time yourself again. Same as you did with the "initial test", you should try to time yourself and to calculate your word per minute rate now. If it stays the same (and this includes 25 words more or less than your first timing too), you are probably too concerned about comprehension. However, as you will later see, comprehension will suffer throughout the speed learning process (this is one of the main reasons why you should practice on less "serious" books).It is natural that you don't understand as much as you would like to, especially at first, when you are just picking up these techniques. Stop worrying and start reading!

Furthermore, another reason why your speed may have stayed the same could be connected to the mechanical activity of picking up the keywords or the chunks of words. Let it go, relax a bit and you will see that you will be able to pick them up naturally as you move along.

If your reading speed drops, it is probably because you are thinking too much. Yes, thinking too much can be hurtful when it comes to speed reading. Instead of focusing on the text, your mind will probably wander to questions such as *"Is this a keyword?"* or *"Is this a good chunk of words"*? If you are doing this and you catch yourself in the moment, make sure you try not to repeat it. Bear in mind, speed reading will feel a bit mechanical at first, but that's perfectly normal because speed reading *is* mechanical, at least up to a certain point.

For those of you whose speed went up, congratulations! You have found a method that works for you and that should get you on the "right" path when it comes to your reading speed.

Scanning

Scanning and skimming are two methods you are probably more than familiar with. While most of the people out there will mistake skimming with scanning (and the other way around too), the truth is that the two of them are quite different at their very core.

Scanning is the process of searching for something specific. If you want an analogy you are likely very close to, think of the way you search for something on Google. You enter a particular word or phrase and you search for something very specific ("plane ticket Rome-New York", for example).

Scanning can be useful when you don't want to read an entire text just to find that one bit of information you need. Some of the pacing methods described before can be very helpful when you are scanning for a particular piece of information. They include left pointing, right pointing, center pointing and card pointing as well.

Skimming

As mentioned before, skimming and scanning are not one and the same thing – but it happens very frequently that people actually use them at the same time! Put in simpler words, skimming is the action through which you are picking up the main ideas in a text (and not just one idea).

If you want another analogy you might be familiar with, think of the way in which you read a webpage. At first, you most likely search for the main ideas (usually given by the headlines and sub-headlines). Then, if you find it interesting, you will read the entire page after having "scanned" Google for your particular keyword of interest.

Skipping

Unless you really want to, you don't have to actually read everything once you have found what you need. You can simply skip over and move to the next interesting thing. This works especially well with non-fiction, but almost never with fiction (where skipping would translate as "cheating" or "spoiling" the book).

Anticipating

Our brain is "built" in brilliant ways and it is able to anticipate a lot of things. Use this when trying to read faster, but make sure you do this the right way so that you don't miss out on important pieces of information.

Chapter 5: Extra-Tips and Tricks

The previous chapter taught you some of the most important exercises and techniques you need to know in order to become a true speed reader. This chapter is dedicated more to those things that can make the difference between average and "high-speed". Some of these items are not related to the way in which you actually read, but to your environment, to the time you choose to read and to other things that may influence your reading speed. Most of these are external factors, rather than internal.

Yes, external factors can play an important role when it comes to speed reading too and even becoming more aware of these factors will likely increase your speed reading and comprehension. The following tips are related precisely to learning how to manage these issues. Additionally, you'll get some tips on how to pick up information in non-fiction books even before you actually become a speed reader.

Where You Read

Most people read on their couch, on a recliner chair or in their beds, but this is not really beneficial for you if you want to speed yourself up. As we briefly touched on earlier, you should try to find a comfortable place, but you should also make sure you are not too comfortable. Even if your interest in the topic you are reading is very high, there is a very likely chance your body will slow down if you are sitting too comfortably in your chair. Once your body starts to relax, your brain will likely start to relax too. Anyone here use reading as a habit before bedtime? There's nothing wrong with this if you're intent is to read something you're not worried about reading. However, if your intent is to read fast and remember what you're reading choose a stiff chair or sit with your back straight are better options!

Also, choose a room where you are not likely to be disturbed. If you are at work, try to show people that you don't want to be disturbed during your lunch break. You can be creative with this and you will be amazed at how willing people are to not bother you if you need some space.

If you read at home, try to do it in a room where the computer and the TV will not pose any "challenge" or be distracting. If you read at school, avoid the library because it can sometimes be much more distracting than you even realize.

Avoid reading in cafés or in loud places and if you do want to read on the subway, make sure you listen to some music: which brings us to the next topic.

Listening to Music

A lot of people like listening to music while they read, but this is a double-edge sword of which you should be aware. Music can relax you and it can make you pay more attention to what you are reading, but it can also be very distracting.

What music should you be listening to? Generally speaking, music that is non-lyrical. Chill-out music that doesn't have much of an upbeat and classical music work the best (think Mozart, Handel and Bach and not so much Vivaldi or more modern instrumental music). This kind of music relaxes your body and it goes with your heartbeat, which means that it will not be distracting in any way.

What music shouldn't you be listening to? In general, all music that contains lyrics should be avoided. Jazz (even if it doesn't have lyrics) should be avoided as well, since it tends to be distracting. Furthermore, avoid rock, hip-hop, indie music or any other kind of music that may swift your attention from the book to the songs.

Take Care of Your Body

Some people take their bodies and their minds as separate entities, but the truth is, they are very much connected to each other. Eating right and working out can go far when it comes to improving your ability to concentrate and to read faster, so make sure you do these things.

Also, here's something else you may not have known: coffee will not help you concentrate more (and neither will any other caffeinated product out there). You may feel more alert when having coffee or when eating candy, but this is not the kind of long-term energy you need in order to read a book and stay focused. Very soon, your energy will wear out and you will be left more tired than you were before. On the other hand, eating oily fish, nuts, complex carbs and fruits will energize your body and your mind much better for the long term.

Do Your Chores

Doing the dishes, doing the laundry, bathing, eating – all of these things can become distractions while you read, so make sure to do them either before you start reading or simply in the small breaks you take in between the sessions. This way, you will not be thinking of grabbing an apple or a cookie when you have reached your 20th page and you will be able to focus on the reading itself. Being hungry or feeling you should be focused on another task are distractions which will derail your focus from the material you're reading and trying to comprehend. So have your snack before you sit down to read, and complete any pressing tasks, then your mind will be able to focus on the task at hand; reading.

Eliminate Temptations

Living in a high-technology world such as ours comes with its advantages, of course – but it can come with a lot of disadvantages too. One of them is related to the fact that we constantly feel the need to multi-task, no matter what we do.

We are not computers. While there are things we can multi-task successfully (doing the dishes and talking with your spouse, for example), reading is not one of them. Therefore, turn off all the distractions. Keep your smartphone away from you and stop yourself from checking those notifications. Turn off your Facebook, Instagram and Twitter. Turn off the TV. Reading is time you spend with yourself and with your book – nothing less, nothing more!

Chapter 6: Comprehend More

Up until now, we have focused more on the "speed reading" part, and less on comprehension. What stops many people from reading faster (and more) is precisely the fact that they are afraid they will miss out on things and that they will not understand what they are reading.

This fear is perfectly natural. Going through lumps of text with your eyes and not remembering much after reading is not speed reading. It is "speed looking". Put simply, you are just glancing through some words to pass some time – you are not *reading*.

When you first start practicing speed reading, you will find that your comprehension level will drop (sometimes significantly). However, this is the moment when you should *not drop out; Don't Quit!* It is normal to see this happening, but it is important that you realize this is a normal part of the process and that you will regain your comprehension level in time. As speed reading becomes more of a mechanism and less of a conscious act, you will also start to understand more of the things you are reading. So the main point here is to be *patient*. The just keep practicing and the learning process will take its course and you'll soon be reading faster and comprehending more.

There are also other things you can do to improve your comprehension level and increase your ability to remember the information you've read. The ability to remember more of what is read is not just important to those persons who aim at remembering as much information as possible, rather it's important to every reader out there, because it will prevent them from back-skipping.

We'll be discussing techniques to increase your ability to remember what you've read here in this chapter. Some of them may work for you, some may not. Try all of them and see which ones are more suitable for your memory.

Coloring Your Books

No, you don't have to go back to kindergarten and use your crayons to color books. But color is a great way to make your mind memorize more and faster. You have probably tried highlighting your texts before, but it is quite likely that you did not do it in an effective way.

For instance, many people highlight whole sentences, but you shouldn't highlight anything else than keywords and chunks of words. Also, make sure you read a block of text before highlighting it – not doing this will usually lead to you highlighting much more than you need.

Take Notes

Both when reading fiction and when reading non-fiction, taking notes can be very helpful. Some people believe that stopping their reading to jot down their ideas will damage their reading speed, but the truth is that the benefits outweigh the time penalty. For instance, one of the advantages related to this is that you will not have to go back to your whole text when you need that piece of information. Furthermore, it is much more likely that you actually comprehend your text if you take notes on it.

If the book you are reading is yours, then you are free to make these notes in the margins. They will help your brain make faster associations and they will also help you memorize the information better.

If the book you are reading is not yours (borrowed from the library) you will not be able to scribble anything on it. However, you can always use sticky notes in different colors to help you memorize things better. They will act both as a bookmark and as a piece of paper on which you can write your own ideas.

Sometimes, you don't even need to write down full sentences to remember things related to a particular part of your text.

One or two words or even certain signs and symbols can work very well – and this should save you a lot of time!

Fiction Notes

While taking notes on non-fiction is pretty straightforward, many people are confused as to how they can take notes on fiction books. Doing this may be necessary especially if you study literature or if you are particularly interested in an author and his style, so it is definitely worth knowing which are the things you should look for.

Characters and their descriptions tend to be very important in books, so you may want to underline those. Also, symbols that may stand out around the text can give you some extra "juice" when it comes to the book you are reading, so remember to underline them when you spot any.

Read More on a Topic

Unless you are a physician, it is very likely that opening a quantum physics book and speed reading through it will be a waste of time. As mentioned in the very beginning of this book, your background knowledge is extremely important if you want to read faster and understand more of what you are reading.

So, if you are completely new to a topic, make sure to get yourself familiar at least with some basic pieces of information surrounding the subject. In time, you will become more and more acquainted with those notions and you will be able to speed-read books based on them as well.

Comprehension is connected to a lot of things, including those mentioned in this chapter and the previous chapter, but it is not limited to these. As mentioned in the first chapter, there are a lot of things that might be stopping you from reading faster and comprehending more: being tired, not having good eye sight and so on. Take a look at that list again and you may find the cause of your low comprehension level.

Also, remember to assess yourself every once in a while. In school, reading comprehension texts came with a series of questions afterwards, but in real-life no business report and no non-fiction book will "test" you at the end. You should be able to assess yourself and to be honest about it too!

Learn How to Read Non-Fiction

Sure, you learned how to read in school. You can read books, magazines and food labels as well. You can read whatever you want, whenever you want.

However, reading non-fiction is slightly different than reading fiction. When considering fiction you have to follow a plot, characters and other parts that make for a good book. On the other hand, with non-fiction you have to follow the information. You read non-fiction because you are searching for information, and not so much for entertainment. Therefore, take it as such.

Before you start reading non-fiction books on a particular subject, skim through the books you have available and pick the book that seems to be the most comprehensive and the most helpful. Take a look at its table of contents. The great thing about non-fiction is that the titles of the chapters will always give away what they are about, so if you find something you are not particularly interested in, you can simply skip it.

Furthermore, be very much aware of the fact that non-fiction books (good ones at least) have a very precise structure. For instance, the first and the last paragraph in a chapter will always give away most of the information within the chapter. If you are not actually interested in finding out the way in which that information was brought together, you can skip the in-betweens. This works the same with paragraphs as well: their first line will nearly always be a brief summary of what the whole block of text is about.

These things can help you speed-read through non-fiction books even faster than only by using the techniques and exercises described in the previous chapters. Use them wisely though and make sure you know when to stop and read everything!

Retain Information Better

As mentioned in the beginning of this chapter, retention is important when you avoiding back-skipping. Aside from using certain triggers (such as the notes on the margins of the books or highlighting keywords with color), there are other techniques that may help you memorize things better. Here are some of the best ones:

Acronyms

These words are formed from the initial letters of other words. When you have to remember certain complex phrases, this is one of the best ways to do it.

Acrostics

When you have to retain a list with many items, you can also try forming a phrase in which each of the words start with the same letter as a word on your list.

Alliteration

Alliteration is the literary technique that brings together words that start with the same letter. Again, when you want to remember certain features of something, you can try to find words to describe it that start with the same letter.

Loci

This method was used by Roman orators and it is a bit more complex than the aforementioned memory tools. Basically, the orators would imagine their home and they would associate each of the rooms in their home with a point they wanted to make. While they delivered a speech, they were merely passing through each of their "rooms" to mark the main ideas they wanted to emphasize.

Chapter 7: Speed E-Reading: Impossible or Not?

It has been quite some time since eBooks first came to be. Back then, not many people were excited about reading books that did not have actual pages. However, these days, more and more of us are turning toward electronic books, and it's nearly impossible to avoid online materials displayed on screens.

There are many features that make eBooks better than traditional books. They are more portable (you can have thousands of books on a device that weighs no more than a newspaper). They are friendlier to the environment and sometimes, they can even help people read faster.

Sure, they don't have the same "feel" as a traditional book, but with the advances of technology, our tablets and eBook readers have become more and more attractive, even for those passionate about "traditional reading".

You may be reading this book on an electronic device, and therefore are probably more open to the idea of electronic books. Considering this, is there any difference between speed reading on a computer/tablet/eBook reader and a speed reading a traditional book?

No, there isn't much difference. Sure, there are things that will differ a bit, but they are nothing to actually worry about. The following tips should help you adapt your speed reading to the electronic era as well.

Good Looking Text

If you read on a laptop or computer, it is quite possible that the columns of text are much wider than your peripheral vision will be able to catch. Make sure to narrow them down, because this will allow you to increase your on-screen reading speed.

Furthermore, always remember to adjust the fonts of your text until you feel comfortable with them. This can easily be done by zooming in (or out) both on laptops/computers and on mobile devices too.

Pacing

Of course, it might look slightly silly to keep your fingers on your computer screen – and it may even leave fingerprints on the screen. Furthermore, it can be very uncomfortable, as you will probably have to keep your arms raised at an unnatural level.

So, what can you do?

There are some pacing options available for those who read electronic books. For instance, you can use your cursor to trace the text the same way you would with your index finger (either through the right pointing method or through the left pointing one – your choice).

Also, you can select one line and then scroll with the down arrow as well. This will help you "take in" a whole line at once, with as few eye stops as possible so that you also increase your reading speed.

If you feel better highlighting a chunk of text, then you can do that as well. This can be done on all computers and laptops and on most of the mobile devices as well (but here it may depend on the software you use to read the eBook).

Be Comfortable

Same as with reading traditional books, you should make sure you are comfortable enough when you read eBooks too. However, this is not so much about the position of your entire body as it is about the position of your head and eyes.

For instance, your eyes should be as parallel as possible with the computer or laptop. Having your monitor raised too high will be uncomfortable for your eyes and for your neck as well.

Also, you should try to keep your eyes about 18 to 28 inches from the monitor. When reading on tablets and eBook readers, keep your device at a considerable distance as well, the same as you would with a normal book.

Make sure to adjust the brightness and the contrast. Not doing this can make your eyes feel very tired and will also cause them to dry out more quickly. Also, make sure to wear your eye glasses because they will help deflect most radiation and reduce the glare from the screen.

Avoid Even-More-Tempting Temptations

One of the main downfalls with reading on electronic devices is related to the fact that temptations are closer than ever. While reading traditional books you can simply turn off your TV, phone and computer, but when reading electronic books, you are *already* on these devices and this means there is a greater likelihood that you will get lured into the "wonders of the Internet". Facebook, your favorite TV shows and your favorite dance music are all there, one click or one tap away. Might I also suggest you do what you can to turn off all those 'notifications' so that you're not distracted by them. Make sure to resist these temptations and to reward yourself only after you have achieved your reading goal.

Chapter 8: Is Speed Reading For Everything?

In the previous chapters, we've mentioned the fact that you can turn your speed reading "on" and "off" when you want. We also mentioned the fact that this is more than advisable, especially under certain circumstances.

In short, speed reading is not for every type of text. There are types of writing where you will want to take your time to understand things better and there are also types of writing that truly deserve all your attention and time.

Technical Books

Reading books that are highly technical, where everything is about numbers is not something you should do in high speed. Of course, the level of "technicality" of a book can vary according to the person who reads it.

Going back to the example with the physician, he/she would probably believe that a book you find "highly technical" to be just "average" or even "easy comprehension". This is related to the fact that, unlike someone who has been studying particular subjects for his/her entire life, you haven't and it is completely new to you.

If you want to actually understand a very technical book, avoid speed-reading through it, especially in the first phase where you are only getting acquainted with the more basic notions.

Very Old Books

Books that are written in Old and Medium English should not be speed-read. It is more than likely that you will not understand anything (even if you are a native English speaker).

The two most common examples of such books include the Bible and Shakespeare. Aside from the fact that the vocabulary used in these books is "obsolete" and that most of the English speakers are not familiar with most of the words, these books tend to be very "heavy" when it comes to themes, motifs and symbolism. The beauty of Shakespeare does not lie in the plots themselves (as some critics show, he may have "borrowed" those from another writer), but in the complexity of the message behind his plays.

Books You Are Reading for Leisure

If you genuinely enjoy reading novels for relaxation, don't speed read through them. Take your time. After all, even if you know how to walk very fast, you don't always do it when you "go out for a walk", do you?

Philosophy

Philosophy books and, generally speaking, most of the "heavier" books out there should not be speed-read either. You will not understand much of the argumentation behind a philosopher's ideas this way. If you want to quickly get familiar with some philosophy notions, speed-read books *on* the most famous philosophical ideas and not the original ones.

Poetry

There is absolutely no point in reading poetry in high speed, really. Poetry is meant to be full of feelings, language, and beauty and should be something relaxing.

Dialogue and Plays

Dialogues are extremely important in books and they are the essence of plays as well. Reading dialogue in high speed is not very useful, because this is where you should actually slow down to "listen" to the voices of the characters. However, once the dialogue part is done, make sure you turn the "volume" down and continue reading at a higher speed (if you want to, of course).

When considering when to turn on or off this new skill, remember speed reading should not be something that is automatically triggered in your mind, but something you control. You are controlling the skill, not the other way around!

Chapter 9: Keep Practicing and Don't *Ever* Give Up!

This book has been a journey through the basic ideas behind speed reading. As it was mentioned in the beginning, this skill can be priceless for students, business people and for just about anyone out there who has a long list of books he/she wants to read.

Take your time. It will not happen overnight. It will probably take some time before you accommodate your eyes (and then your brain) to reading faster than before. Practice does make perfect and speed reading is no exception.

Always keep in mind the fact that your comfort zone is not where you want to be. Push yourself further – and not just when it comes to this particular skill, but to everything else as well. This is how true performance is achieved: in science, in business, in arts and in sports!

Furthermore, remember to try out all the techniques described in this book. Some of them will work better for you and some of them will not be as great. But, it is important that you experiment as much as possible so that you can settle on those methods that fit you best.

Don't be scared if you see that you don't understand as much when you speed read, especially at first. Remember this is normal and that everyone faces this when they begin speed reading.

Keep yourself focused and determined. Remember your *why*; your reason for learning this new skill. Remind yourself of this if/when you feel discouraged. Push through the hard times. Then think of all the personal benefits this new skill will bring and that you are doing this for you. You are doing this because you want to be at the top of the heap! You want to have as much knowledge in your luggage as it can hold because this is the key to true success in every single field of activity out there!

Don't give up, keep on practicing and when you do want to give up, think of someone inspirational. No one ever achieved anything by quitting when things became difficult. They never gave up, and neither should you!

Appendix

Speed Reading and Comprehension Assessment

Within this section you will find three writing segments that are approximately 700 words long. Each writing segment also has an accompanying test with 10 multiple-choice style questions. Together these are meant to allow you to assess your speed reading and comprehension.

Use one writing segment and accompanying test to assess where you stand as a reader before you apply the techniques discussed within this book. The other two are meant to assess your progress after a considerable amount of 'practice' to see how your speed reading and comprehension has improved.

Now remember not to rush the first assessment test. It's meant to assess your current ability to read and comprehend. Set a timer and read the first writing segment. When done, stop the timer and then answer the accompanying 10 questions.

After you've timed yourself reading one of these exams you can refer to the *Speed Reading Rate* table to find your words-per-minute (WPM) rate. This is the measure of your reading speed, but remember we also want to focus on your comprehension. Apply your score on the exam to find your Effective Words Per Minute (EWPM) to adjust for your comprehension.

Record your scores here to assess your progress:

My Starting   EWPM: _____   Date: _____

My Second   EWPM: _____   Date: _____

My Third   EWPM: _____   Date: _____

Speed Reading and Comprehension Table

SPEED READING RATE

Time (Minutes)	Words Per Minute (WPM)	Effective Words Per Minute (EWPM)									
		10%	20%	30%	40%	50%	60%	70%	80%	90%	100%
1.00	1,447	145	289	434	579	724	868	1,013	1,158	1,302	1,447
1.25	1,158	116	232	347	463	579	695	811	926	1,042	1,158
1.50	965	97	193	290	386	483	579	676	772	869	965
1.75	827	83	165	248	331	414	496	579	661	744	827
2.00	724	72	145	217	289	362	434	507	579	652	724
2.25	643	64	129	193	257	322	386	450	514	579	643
2.50	579	58	116	174	232	290	347	405	463	521	579
2.75	526	53	105	158	210	263	316	368	421	473	526
3.00	482	48	96	145	193	241	289	337	386	434	482
3.25	445	45	89	134	178	223	267	312	356	401	445
3.50	413	41	83	124	165	207	248	289	331	372	413
3.75	386	39	77	116	154	193	232	270	309	347	386
4.00	362	36	72	109	145	181	217	253	289	326	362
4.25	340	34	68	102	136	170	204	238	272	306	340
4.50	322	32	64	97	129	161	193	225	257	290	322
4.75	305	31	61	92	122	153	183	214	244	275	305
5.00	289	29	58	87	116	145	174	202	232	260	289
5.25	276	28	55	83	110	138	165	193	220	248	276
5.50	263	26	53	79	105	132	158	184	210	237	263
5.75	252	25	50	76	101	126	151	176	201	227	252
6.00	241	24	48	72	96	121	145	169	193	217	241
6.25	232	23	46	70	93	116	139	162	185	209	232
6.50	223	22	45	67	89	112	134	156	178	201	223
6.75	214	21	43	64	86	107	129	150	171	193	214
7.00	207	20	41	62	83	104	124	145	165	186	207

59

Speed Reading Assessment Test 1 – Reading Segment

Doomsday for Baseball?

Every year, as a new Major League Baseball season begins, America's pastime has a serious problem. Millions of American kids are ditching baseball and choosing to dedicate themselves to other sports. Reasons for the exodus have ranged from "too slow" to outright "boredom," according to many 13-year-olds like Hank Crone, grandson of a major leaguer and the son of one of the top scouts for the Detroit Tigers.

With 11.5 million athletes of all ages in America, baseball still ranks fourth as the most popular team sport, following behind soccer, softball and basketball. Yet, over the last 16 years, participation in Little League Baseball, an account of about two-thirds of all America's youth sports, has been increasingly dwindling. And there is even more evidence the pace is accelerating.

Figures from 2000 to 2009, for example, show that the number of players aged 7 to 17 playing baseball fell 24%, as reported by the National Sporting Goods Association, an industry trade group. Worries of head injuries and their long-term impact had no effect on youth tackle football, whose participation numbers soared to 21% over the same period, while ice hockey jumped to 38%. The Sporting Goods Manufacturing Association, another sporting trade group, reported baseball's participation fell 12.7% for the entire population.

These declining numbers have many scouts concerned. They feel its altering the talent pool in ways that could have a serious impact on the quality of players available. David Bloom, a scout with the Baltimore Orioles, states, "There are still players, but there aren't the number out there anymore. The great players just don't stand out like they used to."

Executive vice-president of Major League Baseball Tim Brosnan said the dull numbers have prompted the league to do its own study and to revise its own strategy to grow the game. Since 1989, more than $50 million have been spent on building and renovating fields and developing baseball leagues, particularly in urban centers where many kids have essentially abandoned the sport. The league has also opened up youth training camps in Texas and California to instruct players in all areas of the game—including umpiring. Brosnan said that participation in baseball as a youth will increase the likelihood of becoming a fan, which is essential for the league's bottom line.

High school baseball has remained steady with a reported 15,786 programs in the U.S. This number makes baseball the No. 3 sport among boys. Youth sports officials say there's been a slight decrease in the number of ball teams, but mainly because of cutbacks in funding, another contributor to the dwindling numbers.

Little League, which covers players aged 4 to 18, had about two million kids on the roster in the U.S. last year, compared to about 2.5 million in 1996—a significant 25% decline. According to the NSGA, the only spike in youth baseball since the 1990s has come from kids who play more than 50 times a year—an indication that the more children play, the more they choose to specialize. A Little League spokesman said the game is morphing into a more-structure year-round sport that requires costly travel, equipment and lessons.

Parents attribute the decline to the game's languid pace, and the fact that other sports force kids to remain alert. They would rather see their kids moving rather than standing around in the outfield. Parents have also been the cause of baseball fields being razed over in communities across America through their political inactiveness. Many city officials are giving the go-ahead to convert outfields to multi-sport facilities for soccer, football, basketball, tennis and lacrosse.

Soccer has now more players than baseball in the U.S., and the number of kids playing lacrosse has more than doubled in the past decade. Lacrosse programs in American high schools have been surging by about 7% a year.

Len Coleman, former president of Major League Baseball, said baseball's only hope may be to entirely change rules to speed up the game. For instance, he states to get rid of the walk. He believes it slows the game and also lessens opportunities for the best players to hit because rival pitchers get told to walk the other teams' heavy hitters. "Give the batter three strikes and tell the pitcher he's got to throw the ball over the plate," Coleman said. "That ought to liven things up."

Speed Reading Assessment Test 1 – Comprehension Questions

Doomsday for Baseball?

1. How many athletes are currently playing sports in America?

    a. 11.3 million
    b. 11.4 million
    c. 11.5 million
    d. 11.6 million

2. How many percentage points did participation in baseball fall among 7 to 17 year olds between 2000 and 2009?

    a. 24%
    b. 25%
    c. 26%
    d. 27%

3. How many percentages did ice hockey grow between 2000 and 2009?

    a. 35%
    b. 36%
    c. 37%
    d. 38%

4. How many percentages did youth tackle football grow between 2000 and 2009?

    a. 20%
    b. 21%
    c. 22%
    d. 23%

5. Over the last 16 years, what fraction of all youth players in America were playing baseball?

    a. One-half
    b. One-fourth
    c. Two-thirds
    d. Three-fourths

6. Which sport is growing at a rate of 7% annually?

    a. Football
    b. Soccer
    c. Basketball
    d. Lacrosse

7. Which of the following is NOT a contributor to the decline of participating in baseball among America's youth?

    a. Lack of outfields in communities
    b. Decreased school funding
    c. Lack of a talent pool
    d. Slow pace of the game

8. How much has Major League Baseball spent in order to grow the sport of baseball?

    a. $50 million
    b. $40 million
    c. $30 million
    d. $20 million

9. Which sport ranks No. 3 among all boys in the United States?

    a. Soccer
    b. Football
    c. Baseball
    d. Basketball

10. Who was an executive vice-president of Major League Baseball?

    a. Len Coleman
    b. David Bloom
    c. Tom Brosnan
    d. Hank Crone

Speed Reading Assessment Test 2 – Reading Segment

Stash Your Cash!

You need a place to stash your cash, and every financial institution is knocking on your door. Well, let them. Always remember: the choice is about you. Short-term savings account that matches your needs is best. Whatever you choose, make sure you consider the following areas: access, interest, service, and penalties.

You will need easy access to your money. You should ask yourself how often will you need to dip into your account, and does the institution offer any of your preferred methods like online banking, check-writing, ATM or any similar structures.

You need to know how much the institution will pay you for keeping your money, and does the amount you need to keep in the account meets the best rates.

You might require services such as in-person customer service, or you would rather do it yourself to keep low maintenance. Decide on this when making a decision.

Lastly, make sure there are no hidden cost for transferring money or savings, and no exorbitant fees for overdrafting.

It's important to go over some basics of personal finance. It will further help you decide which mechanism is best.

The first is checking accounts. They are meant for transactions, not savings. It is a reason why there isn't much return on interest. Yet, some banks do combine the easiness of checking with the return gained from a money market account. Also, accounts known as "asset management" at brokerage houses are becoming more feature-rich, offering ATM access, unlimited check writing and lower money market rates. As a result, many people are shunning banks in favor of brokers to have more control over their accounts.

There are pros and cons of a checking account. The pros are that your money is accessible through an ATM machine anywhere, a bank branch is usually not far from where you live, and all deposits are insured by the Federal Deposit Insurance Corp. The cons are, as stated earlier, not much earnings on your money and minimum balances and fees.

The second is savings accounts. In the past, savings accounts were the most popular form of short-term savings. Since then, people have become a lot of savvy and began shifting their money into higher-yielding investments. The small amount you earn from a savings account is usually not enough to keep up with inflation.

Still, the pros are that money in savings accounts, just as in checking accounts, are insured by FDIC and fees are often low. A con is that the returns on these types of accounts are very slow.

The third is high-yield bank accounts. They are ideal for paying your monthly bills. They allow you to add or withdraw funds at any time, and your money isn't locked for any certain amount of time. Some have better interest rates than more restrictive investments mechanisms. The best rates are offered by online banks that maintain a low cost by scaling back on frills.

The pros are better rates than most standard bank accounts, and receive the same insurance from FDIC. However, the cons are banks with no ATM access or check privileges make it very difficult to get cash fast, and customers must strategize their cash by transferring money from the online bank to a corresponding brokerage account, which could take up to a five-day delay.

The fourth is certificates of deposits, or CDs. These are debt instruments that mature to a certain percentage. It could take 3 months to 60 months. Most are issued by banks, but they can also be purchased from a brokerage house.

The pros of these are that they are very safe because they too are FDIC insured, and CDs may pay more over the long term. The downside is that your money is off-limits until the CD matures. To get access to your money, you must redeem the CD at the expense of a financial penalty.

Speed Reading Assessment Test 2 – Comprehension Questions

Stash Your Cash!

1. What is a CD?

   a. Certificate of deposit
   b. Certificate of debt
   c. Common deposits
   d. Common debts

2. Which of these is good about a checking account?

   a. They offer high returns
   b. They are good for savings
   c. They are insured
   d. They have minimum balances

3. Which of these is not good about a savings account?

   a. They are insured
   b. The fees are low
   c. They are easy to open
   d. They have poor returns

4. Which of these accounts have access to an ATM?

   a. High-yield account
   b. Checking account
   c. Savings account
   d. CDs

5. Which of these should you consider when choosing a financial institution if you need fast cash?

   a. Access
   b. Interest
   c. Service
   d. Penalties

6. If you want to talk to a banker directly, which of these should you consider in your decision to choose a bank?

   a. Interest
   b. Penalties
   c. Access
   d. Service

7. If you have a question about fees, which of these should you consider in your decision to choose a bank?

   a. Interest
   b. Penalties
   c. Access
   d. Service

8. If you want more money from your bank, which of these should you consider in your decision to choose a bank?

    a. Interest
    b. Penalties
    c. Access
    d. Service

9. How long should it take for a CD to mature?

    a. 2 months
    b. 1 month
    c. 10 years
    d. 5 years

10. Who insures your money when it is deposited in a bank?

    a. FDCI
    b. DFIC
    c. FDIC
    d. IFDC

Speed Reading Assessment Test 3 – Reading Segment

Second Inaugural Address of Abraham Lincoln

Fellow Countrymen:

At this second appearing to take the oath of the presidential office, there is less occasion for an extended address than there was at the first. Then a statement, somewhat in detail, of a course to be pursued, seemed fitting and proper. Now, at the expiration of four years, during which public declarations have been constantly called forth on every point and phase of the great contest which still absorbs the attention and engrosses the energies of the nation, little that is new could be presented. The progress of our arms, upon which all else chiefly depends, is as well known to the public as to myself; and it is, I trust, reasonably satisfactory and encouraging to all. With high hope for the future, no prediction in regard to it is ventured.

On the occasion corresponding to this four years ago, all thoughts were anxiously directed to an impending civil war. All dreaded it; all sought to avert it. While the inaugural address was being delivered from this place, devoted altogether to *saving* the Union without war, insurgent agents were in the city seeking to *destroy* it without war-- seeking to dissolve the Union and divide effects by negotiation. Both parties deprecated war, but one of them would *make* war rather than let the nation survive; and the other would *accept* war rather than let it perish. And the war came.

One-eighth of the whole population were colored slaves, not distributed generally over the Union, but localized in the southern part of it. These slaves constituted a peculiar and powerful interest. All knew that this interest was, somehow, the cause of the war. To strengthen, perpetuate, and extend this interest was the object for which the insurgents would rend the Union even by war, while the government claimed no right to do more than to restrict the territorial enlargement of it. Neither party expected for the war the magnitude or the duration which it has already attained. Neither anticipated that the *cause* of the conflict might cease with, or even before, the conflict itself should cease. Each looked for an easier triumph, and a result less fundamental and astounding. Both read the same Bible and pray to the same God, and each invokes His aid against the other. It may seem strange that any men should dare to ask a just God's assistance in wringing their bread from the sweat of other men's faces, but let us judge not, that we be not judged. The prayers of both could not be answered. That of neither has been answered fully. The Almighty has His own purposes. "Woe unto the world because of offenses; for it must needs be that offenses come, but woe to that man by whom the offense cometh." If we shall suppose that American slavery is one of those offenses which, in the providence of God, must needs come, but which, having continued through His appointed time, He now wills to remove, and that He gives to both North and South this terrible war as the woe due to those by whom the offense came, shall we discern therein any departure from those divine attributes which the believers in a living God always ascribe to Him? Fondly do we hope, fervently do we pray, that this mighty scourge of war may speedily pass away. Yet, if God wills that it continue until all the wealth piled by the bondsman's two hundred and fifty years of unrequited toil shall be sunk, and until every drop of blood drawn with the lash shall be paid by another drawn with the sword, as was said three thousand years ago, so still it must be said "the judgments of the Lord are true and righteous altogether."

With malice toward none, with charity for all, with firmness in the right as God gives us to see the right, let us strive on to finish the work we are in, to bind up the nation's wounds, to care for him who shall have borne the battle and for his widow and his orphan, to do all which may achieve and cherish a just and lasting peace among ourselves and with all nations.

Speed Reading Assessment Test 3 – Comprehension Questions

Second Inaugural Address of Abraham Lincoln

1. How much of the U. S. population were slaves when Lincoln gave this address?

    A. One-tenth
    B. One-eighth
    C. One-seventh
    D. One-fifth

2. Which of the following is true about the address?

    A. It was written by someone else
    B. It was delivered after a major battle
    C. It was shorter than the previous address
    D. It was sanctioned by God

3. What word was used to describe those who perpetuated war?

    A. rebels
    B. conspirators
    C. insurrectionists
    D. insurgents

4. According to Lincoln, which of the following was true?

    A. War was discouraged by both parties
    B. Slaves were one of the many reasons for war
    C. God played no part in the start of the war
    D. The prayers of the people for war were answered

5. According to Lincoln, how long had a "bondsman" imposed his will?

   A. 250 years
   B. 260 years
   C. 270 years
   D. 280 years

6. Both sides of the war

   A. Shared the same prayers
   B. Lost their slaves
   C. Accepted war as the only solution
   D. Prayed to the same God

7. Where did Lincoln give this address?

   A. In a hotel
   B. In a city
   C. From an office
   D. In the countryside

8. Which word best describes Lincoln?

   A. pessimistic
   B. revengeful
   C. determined
   D. cautious

9. How long has the war been raging at the time of this address?

    A. 4 ½ years
    B. 4 years
    C. 3 ½ years
    D. 3 years

10. The interest of the slaveholders were described as

    A. influential and astounding
    B. unrequited and firm
    C. rapacious and ungodly
    D. powerful and peculiar

Speed Reading Assessment Test 1 – Comprehension Questions Answer Key:

Doomsday for Baseball?

ANSWERS

1. C
2. A
3. D
4. B
5. C
6. D
7. C
8. A
9. A
10. C

Speed Reading Assessment Test 2 – Comprehension Questions Answer Key:

Stash Your Cash!

ANSWERS

1. A
2. C
3. D
4. B
5. A
6. D
7. B
8. A
9. D
10. C

Speed Reading Assessment Test 3 – Comprehension Questions Answer Key:

Second Inaugural Address of Abraham Lincoln

ANSWERS

1. B
2. C
3. D
4. A
5. A
6. D
7. B
8. C
9. B
10. D

Your Free Gift

I want to show my appreciation for supporting my work so I've put together a little gift for you.

http://comprehensionspeedreading.gr8.com

Just visit the link above to download it now!

I know you will love this gift.

Thanks!

David A. Daniels

Timber Publishing

Made in the USA
Columbia, SC
27 August 2021